Books in the Linkers series

Homes discovered through Art & Technology
Homes discovered through Geography
Homes discovered through History
Homes discovered through Science

Myself discovered through Art & Technology
Myself discovered through Geography
Myself discovered through History
Myself discovered through Science

Toys discovered through Art & Technology
Toys discovered through Geography
Toys discovered through History
Toys discovered through Science

Water discovered through Art & Technology
Water discovered through Geography
Water discovered through History
Water discovered through Science

Food discovered through Art & Technology
Food discovered through Geography
Food discovered through History
Food discovered through Science

Journeys discovered through Art & Technology
Journeys discovered through Geography
Journeys discovered through History
Journeys discovered through Science

First published 1997 A&C Black (Publishers) Limited
35 Bedford Row, London WC1R 4JH

ISBN 0-7136-4771-X

A CIP catalogue record for this book is available from the British Library.

Copyright © 1997 BryantMole Books

Commissioned photographs by Zul Mukhida
Design by Jean Wheeler

Consultant: Ian Punter, Schools' Adviser (Design Technology and Art), East Sussex

The publishers would like to thank the children in Years 1 and 2 of Meeching Valley C.P. School,
East Sussex who produced the artwork featured on pages 9, 15, 19, 22 and 23, and Judy Grahame
who facilitated and guided its production.

Acknowledgements

Cephas; 10 (top), Chapel Studios; John Heinrich 6 (top), Zul Mukhida 8 (top), 12 (left), 16 (top), Positive
Images; 18 (top), Tony Stone Images; Bruce Ayres 3, Visual Arts Library; 20 and 21 (all), Zefa; 14 (top).

Printed and bound in Italy by L.E.G.O.

Food

discovered through
Art and Technology

Karen Bryant-Mole

Contents

A & C Black • London

Food

All living things need food to stay alive.
Food helps your body grow and
stay healthy.
It gives you the energy to run and play.

This apple is ready to eat.
But many foods have to be cooked
or mixed with other ingredients
before we eat them.

Have you ever thought about the work
that goes into your food before you eat it?
Much of the food in shops has been put
into packets, bottles or tins which look
attractive and are easy to store.

We like to eat different types of food for breakfast, lunch and dinner. Each meal needs to be planned and prepared, so that it tastes delicious and looks good.

This book has some ideas that will help you to explore art, design and technology through food.

Food artists

Chefs are people who work with food to create special and tasty dishes. They are rather like food artists.

Chefs mix ingredients together in different ways to make new recipes.
Sometimes, small things, such as a few drops of sauce or a pinch of spice, can make all the difference to a recipe.

Chefs decide how to cook the ingredients too.
Food can be baked, boiled, roasted, fried or grilled.
They also need to work out how long to cook the food for.

This finished dish is a work of art. The chef has worked with the food to produce a meal that not only tastes good but looks good too.

Pizza

You could try making a dish which is a work of art.

Pizzas are made by spreading a tomato sauce over a pizza base and putting a variety of ingredients on top.
The pizza in the picture on the right has been baked in a special pizza oven.

To design your own pizza, you will need a pizza base, some tomato sauce and some toppings, such as onions, mushrooms and cheese.

Pizzas are only cooked for about 15 minutes, so choose toppings that are either already cooked or that can be eaten raw as well as cooked.
Ask an adult to cook your pizza for you.

Here are some pizzas that are ready to be cooked. Which one would you like to eat?

Menus

These people are in a restaurant. They are looking at a menu, deciding what to have for lunch.
Menus tell customers what food is available and how much it costs.

Why not pretend that you have a restaurant and design your own menu?
First of all, decide what type of restaurant it is going to be. Here are some ideas.

ice cream parlour

tea shop   burger bar

Here are some menus that a group
of children have designed.
Can you work out which menu
is designed for which type
of restaurant?

When you have designed
and made your menu, you
could write a list of dishes
and prices inside.

Tools

This woman is using a potato peeler to cut the skin off a potato.
A potato peeler is a type of tool. Many different tools are used to prepare food.

You could use the tools below to help make some biscuits.
Use the knife to cut the margarine and the sieve to sieve the flour and sugar.

Only use a round-ended knife. Never use a sharp knife.

Use the spoon to mix the ingredients together, the rolling pin to roll out the mixture and the shape cutters to cut out the biscuits.

Why not make some biscuit mixture and create your own biscuits?
Ask an adult to bake the biscuits for you.

When the biscuits have been cooked and cooled, you could decorate them.

My favourite meal

The girl in this picture is eating baked beans on toast.
It's one of her favourite meals. What's your favourite meal?

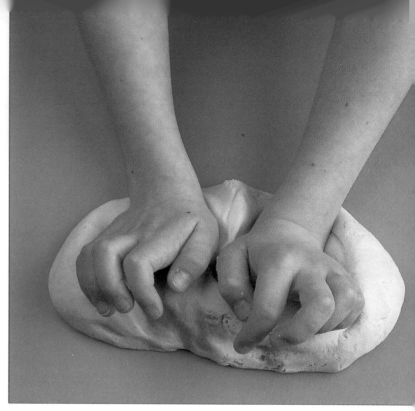

You could use salt dough to make a model of your favourite meal.
To make some salt dough, mix together a cup of plain flour, half a cup of salt and enough water to make a stiff paste.
Then, knead the dough for about five minutes.

Mould your dough into the shape of the foods you like.
Leave the foods in a warm place for a few days to dry out.
Then paint the foods and arrange them on a plate.

Can you tell what these foods are?

Packaging

A lot of the food we buy in shops comes in boxes, bottles or tins.

The wrapping that a food comes in is called its packaging. The words, colours and pictures on the packaging are meant to make you want to buy that food.

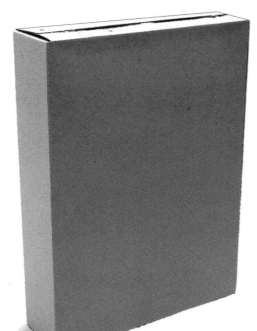

You could design your own packaging for some food.

If you want to make a box, an easy way to do this is to find a packet that is no longer needed and open it up by sliding your finger or a ruler under all the flaps.

Turn the box inside out and stick the flaps down again.

Here are some packaging designs.

Which design do you think is the most eye-catching?

15

Drinks

This girl is enjoying a drink of blackcurrant squash. A cold, refreshing drink is just the thing to cool you down on a hot summer's day.

You could mix together some different ingredients to make your own special drink.
You will need some juices, squashes, fizzy drinks or water and, perhaps, some fruit.

Here are some ideas.

Oranges and Lemons
Mix together some orange juice and lemonade. Decorate the glass with slices of orange and lemon.

Strawberry Fizz
Put some chopped strawberries into a glass. Half fill the glass with grape juice and top up with fizzy water.

Grapefruit and Lime Cooler
Pour some diluted lime squash over a few ice cubes. Add a dash of grapefruit juice and decorate the glass with slices of grapefruit and lime.

Food prints

The prints on the right were made when someone walked across the paving stones, wearing muddy boots.
When something wet is pressed on to a flat, dry surface, the parts that touch may leave a print.

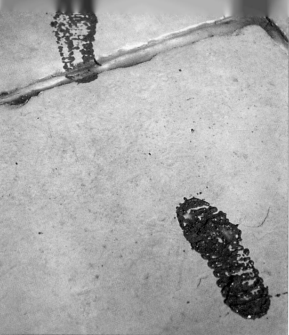

You could use this idea to make prints using food.
Vegetables can make good prints.
Ask an adult to cut the vegetables in half. Dip the flat side of the food in paint and then press it on to paper.

Greengrocers often sell their vegetables in plain paper bags.
A group of children designed these bags for a greengrocer's
shop using vegetable prints.
How many different prints
did they use?

Food in art

Throughout the ages, food has been a very popular subject to paint.
Paintings of objects that do not move, such as food and flowers, are sometimes known as still life paintings.

The painting on the left is called Still Life with Asparagus.
It was painted by an artist called Moillon over three hundred and fifty years ago.

The still life picture below was painted just over a hundred years ago by Van Gogh.
It's called Still Life with Fruit.

Which painting do you prefer?
Is it because you like the food in the painting or because you like the style of the painting?

The still life painting above is called Still Life with Ham.
It was painted about two hundred and fifty years ago by Desportes.

My food pictures

A group of children have made their own still life pictures.
Although they drew or painted the same group of foods,
no two pictures are exactly alike.
A picture is not like a photograph.
A photograph is an exact likeness
of something.
A picture is the artist's own way of
showing what he or she sees.

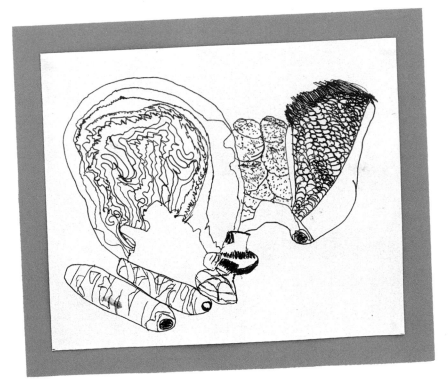

These pictures are pen and
ink drawings.

The pictures above were made with oil pastels.

These pictures were drawn in crayon. Why don't you try creating your own food still life?

Glossary

diluted with water added
greengrocer someone who sells fruit and vegetables
ingredients the parts of a mixture
knead mix with your hands, by pushing and squashing

likeness looks the same as
recipes ways of making food dishes
sieve a tool that separates out the lumps in food such as flour

Index

How to use this book

Each book in this series takes a familiar topic or theme and focuses on one area of the curriculum: science, art and technology, geography or history. The books are intended as starting points, illustrating some of the many different angles from which a topic can be studied. They should act as springboards for further investigation, activity or information seeking.

History

changes have taken place during the past one hundred years, relating to:

- the way food is produced
- how food is transported
- where and how food is bought
- the variety of food available
- the utensils used to prepare food
- how food is cooked
- where food is stored
- how food is preserved
- eating meals

FOOD

key concepts and activities explored within each book

Art and Technology

- food is prepared to make it taste good and look attractive
- chefs are creative with food
- some tools are especially designed for food
- food features in 'still life' works of art
- make a pizza
- design a menu
- print with food
- model a meal
- create a summer drink
- make a still life picture

Science

- all living things need food
- plants make their own food
- foods can be classified into different groups
- we need to eat a variety of foods
- our bodies use different types of food in different ways
- a healthy diet is important
- food travels through our digestive system
- smelling and tasting food involves our senses
- food changes when it is cooked or heated

Geography

- food is usually produced on farms
- there are different types of farm, where different types of food are produced
- climate and land-type determine the food produced
- food can be found in salt water and fresh water
- many foods are processed and packaged in factories
- food is sold in markets, supermarkets and shops
- food can be imported and exported